GW00706194

Reasons
to Smoke

Max Brallier

Running Press
PHILADELPHIA • LONDON

A Running Press® Miniature Edition™
© 2007 by Max Brallier

Printed in China

Library of Congress Control Number: 2007925155

ISBN-13: 978-0-7624-3165-6
ISBN-10: 0-7624-3165-2

This kit may be ordered by mail from the publisher.
Please include $1.00 for postage and handling.
But try your bookstore first!

Running Press Book Publishers
2300 Chestnut Street
Philadelphia, PA 19103-4371

Visit us on the web!
www.runningpress.com

The holidays.

I'm in
a terrible mood.

I'm in
a great mood.

Smoke ring practice.

Those
damn Democrats.

Those
damn Republicans.

No one likes
a quitter.

The end times
are near.

My Siamese twin
can't quit.

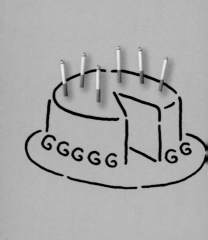

It's my birthday.

I just passed Go!

I'm European.

I'm feeling sort of
Taxi Driver-ish.

It's better than coffee.

It's cheaper than heroin (barely).

I'm wearing
my smoking jacket.

Airport security.

I need
to get rid of that
new car smell.

My high school
yearbook photo.

I like to see myself
as an outlaw.

I'm on my way
to becoming
a crazy cat lady.

I'm not getting
any younger.

It's so vintage.

Gridlock traffic.

My credit card bill.

Someone stole
my iPod.

College loans.

Menthols are
just like smokey
breath mints.

Artificial larynx =
cool robotic voice.

New Jersey.

Little league dads
who just won't
shut the hell up.

I need something
to do with my hands.

My daughter is
a stripper.

I'm in a hot tub
surrounded by
beautiful people.

The price of gas.

Paying all
those taxes feels
so patriotic.

Paris Hilton.

My dog ran away.

My dog died...

Britney Spears.

Goes great with a salad.

Vegetarians.

To calm down.

It's my
stupid human trick.

I have
an oral fixation.

There are so
many cool ashtrays
out there!

I'm drunk.

To piss people off.

It covers up my B.O.

The sun's out!

It's cold out here.

I'm high.

My wife's
cheating on me.

I'm cheating
on my wife.

The IRS.

My partner snores.

I woke up alone.

I've got a sun roof.

Because
the Marlboro Man
is so cool!

Because
the Marlboro Man
is dead.

It's Monday.

⟳

It's Friday.

⟳

Global warming.

The job I have.

The job I had.

I'm a writer.

Geraldo Rivera.

Micro managers.

Incompetent
co-workers.

To make up
for those who don't.

Those awful new *Star Wars* movies.

Lawyers.

I just got laid.

I haven't
gotten laid in three
and a half years.

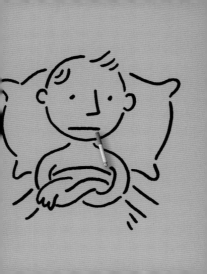

My spouse.

❧

My ex-spouse.

I'm getting
into character.

The in-laws.

Because James Bond
makes it look
so sophisticated!

You gotta die
sometime.

It keeps
my weight down.

❧

Zero trans fat!

My New Year's
resolution:
smoke more!

Spam.

I work in a cubicle.

I love that
Cruella de Ville look

Scientology.

George W. Bush.

Frank Sinatra songs.

Study break.

Party break.

I'm a
Chicago Cubs fan.

Only 3000 more
Marlboro Miles
and I get an official
windbreaker.

It's been a long day.

I've survived three
company layoffs
in two years.

I need butts
to flick at
annoying people.

Because everyone
says I can't.

This book has been bound using
handcraft methods and Smyth-sewn
to ensure durability.

Designed and illustrated by Jason Kayser

Edited by Jennifer Leczkowski.

The text was set in ITC Bookman.